For Your Home

Bathrooms

FOR YOUR HOME

BATHROOMS

Barbara B. Buchholz

FRIEDMAN/FAIRFAX

PUBLISHERS

DEDICATION

To Ed, Joanna, and Lucy

A FRIEDMAN/FAIRFAX BOOK
Friedman/Fairfax Publishers
15 West 26 Street
New York, NY 10010
Telephone (212) 685-6610
Fax (212) 685-1307
Please visit our website: www.metrobooks.com

Library of Congress Cataloging-in-Publication Data available upon request.

ISBN 1-56799-281-1

Editor: Hallie Einhorn
Art Director: Jeff Batzli
Designer: Lynne Yeamans
Layout: Tanya Ross-Hughes
Photography Editor: Wendy Missan
Production Director: Karen Matsu Greenberg

Color separations by Fine Arts Repro House Co. Ltd.
Printed in Hong Kong by Midas Printing Co. Ltd.

3 5 7 9 10 8 6 4 2

Distributed by Sterling Publishing Co., Inc.
387 Park Avenue South
New York, NY 10016-8810
Orders and customer service (800) 367-9692
Fax: (800) 542-7567
E-mail: custservice@sterlingpub.com
Website: www.sterlingpublishing.com

TABLE OF CONTENTS

INTRODUCTION

Ask most homeowners which room is at the top of their wish list to decorate or remodel, and often they'll say it is the bathroom, the most functional and personal space in the home.

Part of the urge is based on pure economics. Unlike adding a swimming pool or redoing a basement recreation room, a refurbished bathroom brings one of the greatest returns for the money invested.

But money provides just part of the explanation. Some of our current fascination with sprucing up and remodeling bathrooms is due to the relative youthfulness of the room as a full-fledged member of a typical home's layout. The bathroom is the new kid on the block. As an indoor space consisting of a sink (called a lavatory in the industry), a tub, and a toilet, it dates back less than one hundred years.

Through much of history, even polite folk had only two less-than-ideal choices: because there was no such thing as indoor plumbing, they could use an outhouse or a chamber pot. For cleansing, they often ventured to their local public baths where they bathed communally, albeit sometimes in luxurious settings.

The first American sink, whose predecessor was a pitcher and basin set on a washstand, dates from the mid-1800s, when sanitary sewers were installed and indoor running water became possible. Credit for this advance is given to Philadelphia architect John Notman, who supplied a home with water via a hydraulic ramp. John Michael Kohler, founder of the huge plumbing conglomerate Kohler Co., sold his first tub to a farmer in 1883. And the first American firm to introduce a vitreous china tank toilet was Eljer Plumbingware Co. in 1907.

But it was not until later in the twentieth century that the bathroom with all three fixtures became part of the typical home. Such a room was usually quite small. At first, not much heed was paid to showcasing the fixtures in more than the most utilitarian way.

The idea of giving a bathroom a distinct style and all the trappings of other rooms did not emerge until the 1920s and '30s, at which point such decorating was done mostly by the wealthy, many of whom were captivated by the large, glamorous bathrooms that Hollywood producers showed in their films. Decades later, after World War II and as suburbs burgeoned nationwide, a larger segment of the population began to enjoy the amenities of the bathroom. The growing demand gave rise to innovations. In 1968, inventor Roy Jacuzzi introduced his now-famous tub with water jets, which was followed by a wave of step-up and step-down whirlpool bathtubs.

Another element that has inspired large numbers of homeowners to refurbish their bathrooms is the fitness and health craze of the last two decades. This trend has created a demand for appealing spots in which to clean up after a workout, particularly among adults with master bathrooms, which lend themselves to being transformed into pampering retreats.

For these rooms, shower manufacturers have copycatted whirlpool designers and debuted larger and more extravagant shower stalls, complete with a variety of showerheads, body sprays, and nozzles. Such showers are often enclosed in sculptural glass-wall designs to provide the feeling of bathing outdoors. The result is a therapeutic relaxation center.

Some homeowners have also come to favor the incorporation of multiple fixtures, the advantages of which they already discovered in their well-equipped kitchens. The goal is similar: to allow two people to use the space simultaneously.

The most lavish of these examples are equivalent to full-size, fully furnished rooms. They boast exercise equipment; comfortable seating; good natural and

Left: ALTHOUGH TILES ARE AMONG THE MOST COMMONLY USED MATERIALS IN BATHROOMS, THEY HAVE THE ABILITY TO CREATE DESIGNS THAT ARE FAR FROM ORDINARY. HERE, A JUMBLE OF MANY TYPES OF TILES BRINGS EXCITEMENT TO A POWDER ROOM, DESPITE A SUBDUED PALETTE. THREE DIFFERENT KINDS OF SCULPTURED BORDER TILES PROVIDE DEPTH AND TEXTURE AS THEY OUTLINE THE SINK AND TRIM THE OVERHANG. LARGER TILES— SOME STRAIGHT UP AND DOWN, SOME ON THE DIAGONAL—COVER THE REST OF THE SPACE, THEIR DIFFERENT HUES AND DIFFERENT POSITIONS DEFYING PREDICTABILITY.

Above: WITH THE HELP OF TROMPE L'OEIL WALLPAPER, THIS CHARMING POWDER ROOM WAS DESIGNED TO LOOK LIKE A BOOK-LINED RETREAT WHERE ONE WOULD WANT TO LINGER. COMBINED WITH A TAFFETA BALLOON SHADE AND AN ANTIQUE STOOL, THE FAUX LEATHER-BOUND VOLUMES GIVE THE ROOM AN OLD-FASHIONED FEELING.

artificial lighting; large windows; abundant storage in medicine cabinets, under vanities, and in closets; and such other amenities as heated towel racks, telephones, televisions, stereo systems, and mirrors equipped with anti-fogging devices.

But master bathrooms are not the only ones targeted for fixing up. Less private bathrooms such as powder rooms or half-bathrooms (often located near a front entry hall or by a kitchen or mudroom), children's bathrooms, and guest bathrooms have followed suit. Even new types of bathrooms have emerged, such as the outdoor bathroom, which consists of a showerhead to wash off sand or dirt and sometimes a soaking tub.

Manufacturers have taken advantage of people's interest in decorating bathrooms by offering fixtures, tiles, wallpapers, and floorings in a plethora of styles, sizes, and colors. They even supply such accessories as soap dishes, toothbrush holders, wastepaper baskets, hooks, and scales in a wide variety of incarnations.

Many of the materials, patterns, and colors have been influenced by trends in other home furnishings. When the lean industrial look took hold in the 1970s, hospital scrub sinks, stainless steel counters, and doctor's cabinets started popping up in home bathrooms. When an interest in the Orient materialized in the 1980s, Japanese-style teak soaking tubs became de rigueur in Far Eastern–inspired bathrooms.

The trend now is clearly not toward a single look, but for designs that share some common denominators with the rest of the home's decor. Bathrooms have become as varied in their style, mood, and size as any other room in the home. Some are quite elegant, with marble floors and antique mirrors to rival the most opulent Roman baths, while others are downright contemporary and funky, with crayon-colored faucets and a rainbow of different-colored tiles covering the walls and floors.

Other bathrooms reflect their settings or owners' interests. A bathroom for a beach house may have tiles with a seashell motif, permanently sunny yellow towels, and soaps shaped like fish. A young child's bathroom may have smaller fixtures complemented by wallpaper borders that teach how to count or to recognize the letters of the alphabet. And the bathroom of a plant aficionado may house a conservatory of greens because the humidity helps certain varieties, such as ferns, thrive.

Not all bathrooms are large and elaborate, however. Some are actually quite small—almost as tiny as those on airplanes and trains. Often, they are made to look larger with mirrors placed on the walls and ceilings.

Decorating a bathroom can be relatively easy these days, thanks to many new and affordable bathroom resources, such as neighborhood design and hardware centers, home furnishings mail-order catalogs, and salvage shops. You may find the perfect antique claw-foot tub and pedestal sink for a fraction of their original value because someone decided they just had to have a computer-programmed whirlpool tub that would allow them to turn on their bathwater while still at the office.

Although redoing a bathroom can exceed many families' budgets, the process need not be so expensive. The secret is to set priorities: decide what you can reuse, what you should discard, and what new features and fixtures you view as most important.

Small Spaces

Not all bathrooms have become large and ultraluxurious. Indeed, the small bathroom remains a necessity in many homes on account of space constraints. Due to the small size of these rooms, a great deal of imagination is often necessary to incorporate all the basic features and to make the spaces look larger and more appealing. The challenge becomes even greater when ceilings are angled because sloping roof lines and when walls jut out creating nooks and crannies, though such architectural elements can be played up to add charm and whimsy.

The smallest type of bathroom has traditionally been the powder room, which is also referred to as a half-bathroom because it excludes a tub. Such rooms are sometimes fashioned out of former closets or from space borrowed from other rooms. Often, the sink and toilet are scaled down in size so that they will fit into the compact space. The smaller scale of these rooms, though, does not mean that they have to be any less attractive than their larger counterparts. In fact, many demonstrate a tremendous amount of ingenuity. And they come in all different styles, from casual to dressy, depending on the location in the home and the rest of the decor.

Those bathrooms adjacent to the front hallway are often rather formal, showing off fancy paint finishes or wallpapers, as well as elegant marble or wood floors. Small bathrooms near the kitchen, back hall, or family room, however, are often designed to sustain harder wear and tear, so they tend to have floors, wall coverings, and accessories of a more practical nature.

Opposite: Framed black-and-white photographs of celebrities accent one wall in a film buff's powder room. A large mirror duplicates the favorite images and expands the tiny space, which is outfitted with a small pedestal sink and a sturdy but basic schoolroom-type armchair that serves as an extra towel rack. The walls are painted with a crackle finish to suggest age. **Above:** Evoking the feeling of a garden, the walls in this bathroom were painted to resemble blocks of stone, then accented with painted trailing vines and flowers. Café curtains bearing a similar floral motif, a basket boasting a dried arrangement, and a framed botanical print contribute to the bucolic feeling. These finishing touches also add soothing bits of color to the mostly monochromatic space.

Left: THIS ANTIQUE STAINLESS STEEL BOWL, WHICH HAS MORE AESTHETIC THAN MONETARY VALUE, HAS TAKEN ON A NEW LIFE AS A SINK BASIN IN A POWDER ROOM. PAIRED WITH A STRIKINGLY CONTEMPORARY FAUCET AND PLACED ATOP AN OLD WOOD TABLE, THE BOWL IS PART OF AN ECLECTIC MIX THAT FORMS AN ATTRACTIVE THREE-DIMENSIONAL STILL LIFE.

Opposite: A CURVING CABINET CRAFTED FROM MAPLE WAS ELEVATED TO ART STATUS WHEN ITS FRONT WAS PAINTED WITH A ROMANESQUE-TYPE GARDEN DESIGN. THE MARBLE COUNTERTOP AND BACKSPLASH PICK UP THE DEEP GREEN-GRAY TONES, WHICH ARE ALSO ECHOED IN THE LEAFY BORDER OF THE MIRROR.

Opposite: BY ANGLING A SCALED-DOWN SINK IN A CORNER, THE OWNERS OF THIS INVITING HALL BATHROOM WERE ABLE TO SQUEEZE A TOILET INTO THE COMPACT SPACE. BRASS FIXTURES, GILT FRAMES, AND THE YELLOWISH BACKGROUND OF THE FLORAL-PATTERNED WALLPAPER AND MATCHING SINK SKIRT CAST A GOLDEN WARMTH UPON THE AREA. ACCENTED BY A CLASSIC BRASS CANDLESTICK AND A SMALL BOUQUET OF FRESH FLOWERS, THE ROOM HAS AN ALMOST ROMANTIC FEEL-ING. THE USE OF A SOLID, DARK HUE ON THE DADO, CEILING, AND CURTAIN LINING PROVIDES A GROUNDING SENSE OF CONTRAST. **Above left:** SOMETIMES A "BATHROOM" CAN CONSIST OF JUST A SINK IN A HALLWAY, AS IN THIS ALCOVE OFF A BEDROOM. AN OLD, PAINTED-WHITE WOODEN TABLE WAS GIVEN A NEW TOP, INTO WHICH A SIMPLE WHITE BOWL WAS PLACED. A MONOGRAMMED HAND TOWEL, AN OLD-FASHIONED TOWEL HOOK, A LARGE MIRROR, AND A VASE PERENNI-ALLY FILLED WITH FLOWERS ENHANCE THE ICONOCLASTIC SETTING. **Above right:** UNORTHODOX IN ITS PAIRINGS, THIS POWDER ROOM BOLDLY DEFIES CONVEN-TION. SIDE MIRRORS FROM A TRUCK SCREAM MODERN SOCIETY WHILE ORNATE CRYSTAL CHANDELIERS HARKEN BACK TO A QUIETER TIME. THE LAVATORY, CONSISTING OF A LARGE, WHITE CHINA BOWL MOUNTED ATOP A MARBLE COUNTER RATHER THAN SUNK INTO IT, ALSO PRESENTS AN UNUSUAL TWIST. THE WALLS AND FLOOR WERE DELIBERATELY LEFT AS A MONOCHROMATIC EXPANSE SO AS NOT TO INTERFERE WITH THE UNIQUE COLLECTION OF FIXTURES AND DECORATIVE OBJECTS.

Above: CONNOTING CLEANLINESS AND FRESHNESS, THE COLOR WHITE CREATES A WHOLESOME AIR IN THIS SMALL WOOD-LINED BATHROOM. AIRY BRACKETS RESEMBLING GARDEN LATTICES FURTHER CONTRIBUTE TO THE NATURAL FEELING OF THE ROOM, WHILE AT THE SAME TIME SERVE THE HIGHLY FUNCTIONAL PURPOSE OF SUPPORTING NECESSARY SHELVES. A COLLECTION OF OLD BLUE AND GREEN BOTTLES FOUND AT ROADSIDE SHOPS RESTS ON ONE OF THESE SHELVES, ADDING A GENTLE SPLASH OF COLOR TO THE SURROUNDINGS. **Opposite:** FILLED WITH A SENSE OF NOSTALGIA, THIS QUAINT WASHROOM, CARVED OUT OF A BEDROOM CORNER, BOASTS A CHINA BOWL AND PITCHER ATOP A PAINTED WOODEN CABINET. CHEERY BLUE-AND-WHITE STRIPED TICKING COVERS THE BASE OF THE CABINET, GIVING THE ROOM A SUMMERY AIR YEAR-ROUND. DARKER BLUE AND WHITE STRIPES FLANK THE FULL-LENGTH MIRROR AND GRACE THE AREA RUG, WHICH FEELS COMFORTING TO BARE FEET ON COLD MORNINGS. ABOVE THE MIRROR, A FRIEZE FROM A DEMOLISHED BUILDING ADDS PANACHE.

Below: IN THIS TINY ATTIC BATHROOM, AN OLD WOODEN CABINET WAS FITTED TO HOUSE A SINK AND THEN TOPPED WITH A STONE SLAB, A SMALLER VERSION OF WHICH RESTS ATOP THE BACK OF THE PIECE. THE CASUAL MOOD OF THE ROOM WAS PLAYED UP BY USING A SIMPLE, OLD WOODEN MEDICINE CABINET, TERRA-COTTA FLOOR TILES, AND PALE SHADES OF PAINT. A GREEN LINE RUNNING ALONG THE WALL ECHOES THE SLOPE OF THE ROOF.

Opposite: A NARROW BATHROOM WITH FIFTIES-STYLE TILING WAS SPRUCED UP WITH MINIMAL EFFORT AND WITHOUT EXPENSIVE ARCHITECTURAL CHANGES BY INCORPORATING SOME HANDSOME YET SIMPLE PIECES INTO THE SPACE: A CRISP WHITE PEDESTAL SINK WITH DECKS AND TOWEL RACKS ON BOTH SIDES, A LARGE MIRROR WITH A FANCIFUL PAINTED CURLICUE DESIGN, A LARGE OVERSCALE WIRE WASTEBASKET, AND A RATTAN TABLE THAT SERVES AS A RESTING SPOT FOR EXTRA TOWELS AND FRESH BLOOMS. STARLIKE ACCENTS ON THE FLOOR JAZZ UP THE SPACE. **Above:** INSTEAD OF IGNORING THE STEEP PITCH OF THIS BATHROOM CEILING, THE DESIGNER USED IT TO HIS ADVANTAGE BY INTRODUCING AN ENORMOUS GEOMETRIC MIRROR THAT TAKES UP ALMOST THE ENTIRE WALL. THE HEXAGONAL SHAPE IS REPEATED IN THE SINK, WHICH IS COVERED WITH BLUE-TINTED GLASS THAT ECHOES THE DISPLAY SHELVES.

Above left: THIS POWDER ROOM OFF A FRONT HALL DAZZLES GUESTS WITH ALL ITS GLITZ AND GLAMOUR. EXUDING OPULENCE, A BLACK MARBLE COUNTERTOP SITS REGALLY ATOP A RICHLY HUED MAHOGANY CABINET AND GRACEFULLY HOUSES A GOLD-TONED SINK. ADORNED BY BRASS-AND-CRYSTAL FIXTURES, THE SHINY SINK MAKES WASHING ONE'S HANDS SEEM LIKE A DECADENTLY LUXURIOUS AFFAIR. A GOLD-LEAFED MIRROR FLANKED BY ELEGANT SCONCES BECKONS THE VISITOR TO PRIMP, CREATING A CAPTIVATING FRAME FOR THE IMAGE IT REFLECTS. **Above right:** THIS SMALL POWDER ROOM RECEIVES ITS UNUSUAL APPEAL VIA A COMBINATION OF DETAILS: A MATCHING SET OF OLD-FASHIONED FRAMES MADE OF WOOD AND TIN, A NARROW BACKSPLASH OF TRIANGULAR AND DIAMOND-SHAPED TILES IN SHADES OF ROSE AND GRAY, AND AN ANTIQUE JAPANESE BOWL THAT TAKES THE PLACE OF A TRADITIONAL BASIN. THE TRIANGULAR DESIGN OF THE COUNTER-TOP, ECHOED BY THE ROSE TILES, IS AN EFFECTIVE MEANS OF SAVING SPACE. **Opposite:** HERE, AN OLD PEDESTAL WITH DEEP CARVINGS AND RELIEFS HAS BEEN TRANSFORMED INTO AN INNOVATIVE SINK THAT WILL KEEP GUESTS TALKING. SPORTING A HIGH-NECKED FAUCET, WHICH WAS OBTAINED FROM A HOSPITAL SUPPLY SOURCE, THE SINK HAS AN ELONGATED LOOK THAT MAKES THE REST OF THE ROOM SEEM LARGER. THIS SPATIAL ILLUSION IS FURTHER ENHANCED BY A FULL-LENGTH MIRROR POSITIONED STRATEGICALLY BEHIND THE SINK. MAHOGANY PANELING COVERS THE WALLS AND CEILING, ENVELOPING THE SPACE WITH A MAJESTIC TONE.

Opposite: IN SPITE OF ITS SMALL SIZE, THIS APARTMENT BATHROOM WAS GIVEN AN ELEGANT MAKEOVER. A SMALL ORIENTAL RUG WAS PLACED ON TOP OF THE ORIGINAL VINYL FLOOR; A GOTHIC-INSPIRED CHAIR WITH AN ELABORATE SEAT COVER WAS BROUGHT IN FOR APPLYING MAKEUP; AND A NARROW SET OF SHELVES WAS TUCKED INTO A CORNER TO KEEP FAVORITE PICTURES AND READING MATTER HANDY. SMALL PHOTOGRAPHS OF FAMOUS STATUES ARE DISPLAYED ARTFULLY AROUND THE ROOM, TRANSFORMING IT INTO A GALLERY OF SORTS. **Right:** BOASTING VIBRANT RED FLOWERS AGAINST A BLACK BACKGROUND, THE WALLPAPER IN THIS ORNATE POWDER ROOM MAKES A DRAMATIC STATEMENT. EQUALLY DRAMATIC ARE THE RICHLY CARVED GOLD MIRROR AND ELABORATE CRYSTAL CHANDELIER, WHICH GIVE THE SMALL SPACE A PALATIAL FEEL.

STYLE

The styles of bathrooms vary tremendously. There are those with a period look, incorporating fixtures that come from a certain country or time; contemporary spaces made to look old with the addition of antique claw-foot tubs and washstands; and ultramodern designs boasting sculptural see-through showers, platform tubs, sleek updates of traditional pedestal sinks, and walls of glass that open to the outdoors.

The style selected often reflects the decor of the rest of the home, though there is no rule of thumb that says French provincial or English country homes must have similarly styled bathrooms. In fact, it is often more exciting to introduce an element of surprise and create a potpourri of flavors. Today, many of the rooms in a home manifest a blend of traditions, and the bathroom is no exception. For instance, an old claw-foot placed in the center of a highly modern space can have a dynamic impact.

One important criterion to heed, though, is that there be some uniformity in scale, color, pattern, or texture when selecting fixtures, fittings, materials, and accessories. Such elements can provide a powerful sense of continuity regardless of whether the bathroom adheres to a specific style or boasts an eclectic mix.

Practical considerations must also be taken into account. Area rugs, comfortable upholstered chairs, fine wall coverings, and billowy curtains can create traditional romance, but owners should beware that water and humidity may not be kind to certain materials.

Opposite: THE MOORISH-STYLE ARCH IN THIS LARGE SUBURBAN BATHROOM INSPIRED THE ROOM'S ROMANTIC CASBAH FEELING. THE EFFECT WAS COMPLETED WITH A MIX OF SOLID AND PATTERNED GREEN-AND-WHITE TILES REMINISCENT OF THOSE POPULAR IN SPANISH-INFLUENCED NORTH AFRICAN DESIGN. DESERT-COLORED TILES PAVE THE FLOOR, SOFTENED IN FRONT OF THE TUB BY A SMALL ORIENTAL RUG. **Above:** THE SPARENESS OF AMISH CABINETRY WAS THE INSPIRATION FOR THIS BATHROOM'S DESIGN, WHICH ALSO HAS HINTS OF SCANDINAVIAN SIMPLICITY IN ITS STREAMLINED PEDESTAL SINK, PALE WOOD DADO, AND WHITE UPPER WALLS. BEIGE TILES FORMING A SUBTLE HONEYCOMB PATTERN ON THE FLOOR MAINTAIN THE NEUTRAL PALETTE, AS DOES THE WALNUT STORAGE UNIT. ASIDE FROM HOUSING TOWELS AND LINENS, THIS FREESTANDING UNIT CREATES A BARRIER THAT ENSURES PRIVACY FOR THE MORE PERSONAL AREA OF THE BATHROOM.

Above: MARIE ANTOINETTE WOULD HAVE LOVED THIS CAST-IRON TUB WITH ITS MATTE BLACK EXTERIOR AND GOLD-PLATED FEET. THE DECIDEDLY FRENCH MOOD IS INTENSIFIED BY A MARBLE FIREPLACE, AN ANTIQUE ARMOIRE (WHICH CONCEALS ENTERTAINMENT EQUIPMENT), AND WALLPAPER DISPLAYING A DELICATE, AIRY DESIGN. THE GLEAMING WOOD FLOOR IS GRACED BY TWO SMALL TILED SECTIONS, WHICH PROVIDE WATERPROOF SURFACES AND RESEMBLE AREA RUGS. **Opposite:** DECKED OUT IN A FRENCH STYLE THAT BEARS A FARMHOUSE-CUM-GARDEN FEELING, THIS BATHROOM INCLUDES A TUB WITH AN UNUSUAL LATTICE SURROUND. A PALE YELLOW-AND-BLUE FLORAL PRINT THAT ADDS TO THE PROVINCIAL TONE IS USED FOR THE SINK SKIRT, THE BALLOON SHADES, THE HAMPER LINING, AND EVEN THE TRIM OF THE UPHOLSTERED CHAIR. TO HEIGHTEN THE PASTORAL AMBIENCE, THE WALLS ARE COATED IN A PALE SHADE OF ROBIN'S-EGG BLUE.

Left: ASIDE FROM ITS OLD-FASHIONED-STYLE SINK, THIS BATHROOM COULD EASILY PASS AS AN ART-FILLED ENGLISH STUDY. A SMALL READING STAND SHOWCASES CURRENT PERIODICALS, WHILE A TABLE WITH AN ORNATE GILDED PEDESTAL DISPLAYS FAVORITE BOXES AND FRESH FLOWERS. IMPOSING GLASS CANDLESTICKS STAND TALL ON EITHER SIDE OF THE SINK AND, TOGETHER WITH AN ASSORTMENT OF DELICATE VIALS FILLED WITH COLORFUL LIQUIDS, CREATE THE IMAGE OF A SHRINE. STAINED GLASS, WHICH PICKS UP THE COLORS OF THE FLOOR TILES ARRANGED IN AN ELABORATE NEAR EASTERN DESIGN, FURTHER CONTRIBUTES TO THE ALMOST SPIRITUAL AMBIENCE.

Above: BATHED IN PALE BLUE AND ACCENTED WITH WHITE TRIM, THIS EXQUISITE BATHROOM LOOKS LIKE A PACKAGE FROM TIFFANY. THE CLAW-FOOT TUB, EMBRACED BY A STATELY ARCH, WAS PAINTED TO MATCH THE WALLS, WHICH CREATE A SUBDUED BACKDROP FOR THE ASSORTMENT OF COLLECTIBLES. THE LAVATORY IS HOUSED IN AN OLD BAR; A WICKER AND BAMBOO CHAIR IS PAIRED WITH AN ANTIQUE DRESSING TABLE; AND WALL-TO-WALL CARPETING IS ACCENTED WITH A SMALL NEEDLEPOINT RUG.

Below: Although the decor of this bathroom off a guest room seems somewhat spare, the amenities give visitors much more than a cold morning cleansing. A feeling of rejuvenation pervades the space, thanks to a new incarnation of a Victorian tub. Combined with a contemporary-style overscale mirror, crisp white wainscoting, and bare double-hung windows, the piece imbues the room with a fresh look.

Opposite: The owners of a large home could not resist turning an extra bedroom into a luxurious master bathroom, complete with a claw-foot tub displayed proudly between two grand windows that act as a frame. Other creature comforts include a sumptuous armchair, fully stocked built-in shelves, and a glorious view of an English wildflower garden. A weathered antique mirror, flanked by light fixtures of the same era, blends in readily with the old-fashioned tub to create a traditional tone.

Above: A tiny courtyard off this master bathroom provides a wonderful garden view from the traditional cast-iron tub. Sheer shades are rarely pulled down, except when the sun is too strong or when the bather wishes to block views.

Opposite: THE ECLECTIC BLEND IN THIS CHARMING BATHROOM HAS AN OVERALL TRADITIONAL TONE, THANKS TO THE EXTENSIVE USE OF DARK WOOD, WHICH ENGULFS THE TUB, FRAMES THE MIRROR, AND COVERS THE FLOOR. BUT A TRADITIONAL TONE DOES NOT HAVE TO SEEM ORDINARY, AS EVIDENCED BY THE NOVEL TOUCHES THAT ABOUND IN THE SPACE. SQUARE CUTOUTS FORM AN ORIGINAL, EYE-CATCHING FRINGE ON THE VALANCE, WHILE DIFFERENT FABRIC BEARING A SIMILAR LOOK DRESSES UP AN OLD PEDESTAL SINK. A COLLECTION OF POTTERY THAT ONE WOULD EXPECT TO SEE IN A LIVING ROOM RESTS ON THE BROAD LEDGE OF THE TUB, RESIDING SIDE-BY-SIDE WITH BOTTLES OF BATH OILS—THE MORE COMMON BATHROOM INHABITANTS. **Above:** HERE, A SITTING ROOM OFF A MASTER BEDROOM WAS TRANSFORMED INTO AN ENTICING BATHROOM. WITH ITS HARDWOOD FLOOR, HOOKED RUGS, PAINTED WOODEN MOLDING, ANTIQUE WOODEN CHAIR, AND STAINED GLASS WALL HANGINGS, THE SPACE RETAINS ITS SITTING-ROOM CHARACTER, MAKING IT A RELAXING SPOT FOR A BATH.

Above left: PAINT WAS USED TO FRESHEN UP THIS SIMPLE BATHROOM IN A COST-EFFECTIVE WAY. WALLS AND WOODWORK WERE PAINTED A CLEAN, CRISP WHITE, AND A FLORAL DESIGN IN COUNTRY TONES WAS STENCILED NEAR THE CEILING, CREATING AN EFFECTIVE SUBSTITUTE FOR MOLDING. A SIMILAR PATTERN WAS STENCILED AROUND THE PERIMETER OF THE DARK GREEN PAINTED FLOOR, WHICH PREVENTS THE PREDOMINANTLY WHITE ROOM FROM APPEARING WASHED OUT. ALSO BREAKING UP THE VISUAL MONOTONY IS A SIMPLE BLACK VASE POSITIONED ON THE DECK OF THE TUB. **Above right:** TO WARM UP THIS BATHROOM— BOTH PHYSICALLY AND AESTHETICALLY—A COLORFUL ORIENTAL RUG WAS PLACED OVER THE CERAMIC TILE FLOOR. THE RUG'S DEEP RED HUES AND SOFT TEXTURE COMBINE WITH THE RICH WOODS OF THE CABINETS AND PANELING TO MAKE THE LARGE SPACE SEEM MORE COZY AND INTIMATE. BLACK AND BEIGE TILES RUN AROUND THE PERIMETER OF THE FLOOR, CREATING A HANDSOME BORDER FOR THE RUG. SOOTHING BLUE-GRAY TRIM ACCENTS THE SHOWER STALL, WHICH INCLUDES A BENCH AND MIRROR. **Opposite:** TO GIVE THIS BATHROOM THE REFRESHING LOOK OF A SPRING DAY, THE UPPER PORTION OF THE WALLS WAS PAPERED WITH AN AIRY BLUE-AND-CREAM PATTERN. THE DADO, HOWEVER, WAS PAINTED SOLID WHITE IN ORDER TO PROVIDE A VISUAL BREAK BETWEEN THE DISTINCT DESIGNS OF THE WALLPAPER AND TILED FLOOR. A SIMPLE TRELLIS-PATTERNED SHOWER CURTAIN AND MATCHING VALANCE OFFER FURTHER IMAGES OF SPRING WITH THEIR FLORAL DESIGNS—YOU CAN PRACTICALLY SMELL THE DELICATE BLOOMS.

Opposite: CREATING AN AMBIENCE OF TRANQUILITY, THIS MODERN VERSION OF A JAPANESE SOAKING TUB TRANSPORTS THE BATHER TO THE ORIENT. A SHOJI SCREEN OPENS TO REVEAL THE SOOTHING GREENERY OF AN OUT-DOOR GARDEN AND CLOSES TO MAINTAIN PRIVACY. **Right:** WITH A REFRESHINGLY SIMPLE DESIGN, THIS BATHROOM DEMON-STRATES HOW NATURE CAN BE BROUGHT INDOORS, EVEN INTO A UTILITARIAN SPACE. AN UNOB-STRUCTED WALL OF GLASS MAKES IT SEEM AS THOUGH THE PEACEFUL GARDEN BEYOND IS ACTUALLY PART OF THE BATHROOM. TWO FACING MIRRORS MULTIPLY THE IMAGE, THEREBY EXTENDING THE SERENITY AND MAKING THE NARROW SPACE SEEM EXPONENTIALLY LARGER. A SLATE FLOOR ADDS TO THE OUT-DOOR SENSATION.

Opposite: WHEN A LOVER OF CONTEMPORARY ART ASKED THAT HER BATHROOM REFLECT THAT APPRECIATION, THE ARCHITECT MET THE CHALLENGE IN SEVERAL WAYS. THE DOOR LEADING INTO THE ROOM WAS DESIGNED WITH A GRID REMINISCENT OF A PIET MONDRIAN PAINTING, AND A THREE-DIMENSIONAL SCULPTURE OF CHUNKY FREE-FORM TRIANGLES WAS POSITIONED TO SERVE AS A SHOWER CURTAIN. THE REST OF THE ROOM WAS DELIBERATELY LEFT SPARE TO ALLOW THE "ART" TO STAND OUT.

Above: CONTEMPORARY IS SOMETIMES RELATIVE, AS IN THIS EARLY RANCH HOUSE, WHICH WAS CONSIDERED QUITE MODERN AT THE TIME IT WAS BUILT YET BECAME RATHER DATED OVER THE YEARS. THE NEW OWNERS KEPT THE ORIGINAL FIXTURES, BUT FRESHENED THE ROOM WITH A NEW COAT OF YELLOW PAINT IN A FAUX LEATHER FINISH THAT ECHOES THE WOOD DRAWERS AND TRIM. FURTHER ADDITIONS INCLUDE A NARROW WHITE WINDOW SHADE AND A PAIR OF MASSIVE ROUND MIRRORS.

Above: MULTIPLE LEVELS SEEM APROPOS IN A BATHROOM THAT MANIFESTS A CELESTIAL THEME WITH THE HELP OF A GIANT CIRCULAR LIGHT FIXTURE ADORNED BY TINY STARS. THE SAME TRAVERTINE IS USED ON THE FLOORS, WALLS, AND TUB SURROUND IN ORDER TO MAINTAIN A SENSE OF CONTINUITY BETWEEN THE DIFFERENT LEVELS. BLACK ACCENTS IN THE FORM OF BORDER TILES, DECORATIVE COLUMNS, MOLDING, AND THE INSIDE OF THE WHIRLPOOL TUB ADD DRAMA SUITABLE FOR AN INTERPLANETARY VOYAGE.

Right: GLASS BRICKS HAVE ENJOYED A REVIVAL BECAUSE OF THEIR ABILITY TO PROVIDE PRIVACY WHILE LETTING IN LIGHT. HERE, THEY GRACEFULLY CAMOUFLAGE THE TOILET CUBICLE, DEFTLY SECTIONING IT OFF FROM THE REST OF THE SPACE. AMPLE WHITE STORAGE TOPPED BY A SLEEK BLACK MARBLE COUNTERTOP ALLOWS THE SPACIOUS RETREAT TO SERVE AS A DRESSING ROOM AND FREES UP DRAWER SPACE IN THE BEDROOM. RECESSED LIGHTING TAKES THE PLACE OF OBTRUSIVE FIXTURES, THEREBY ADDING TO THE SMOOTH LOOK OF THE CONTEMPORARY SPACE.

Left: THE PORTHOLE-SHAPED LIGHTS AND THE WOODEN CABINETRY AND TRIM WERE INSPIRED BY A LOVE OF BOATS. THE WOOD IS COMPLEMENTED BY A MARBLE COUNTERTOP AND TILE FLOOR THAT ADD SIMILAR BUT DISTINCT EARTHY SHADES. A GLASS BRICK WALL SEEN THROUGH THE MIRROR ADDS DIMENSION AND SCREENS THE BATHING AREA. **Opposite:** WHILE THE SHAPE AND FITTINGS OF THIS TUB ARE TRADITIONAL, ITS STAINLESS STEEL FEET AND CENTRAL PLACEMENT IN THE BATHROOM LEAVE NO DOUBT THAT THE SPACE BELONGS TO SOMEONE WITH A SENSE OF DARING. A LONG, NARROW MIRROR THAT APPEARS TO REST PRECARIOUSLY ON A SMALL LEDGE ADDS TO THE FEELING OF RISK, EVEN THOUGH THE MIRROR IS ACTUALLY FIRMLY ANCHORED. BUILT-IN STORAGE, DEVOID OF ANY DISTRACTING HARDWARE, LINES THE WINDOW WALL.

Right: ON THE TOP LEVEL OF A SECLUDED MODERN BEACH HOUSE, A LARGE SHOWER IS JUST BARELY SCREENED BY TWO SHORT WALLS OF FROSTED GLASS THAT SERVE PRIMARILY TO RESTRICT THE SPRAY OF WATER. AN IMMENSE PICTURE WINDOW PROVIDES A GLORIOUS VIEW OF THE OCEAN WHILE CLEANSING.

ADDING COLOR

The color or combination of colors selected for a bathroom is as important in creating a mood as are the style and period of the fixtures and accessories. Among the key decisions is whether to go with a monochromatic or mixed palette. The next step is to decide what type of color or colors to use.

Manufacturers of bathroom-related items have developed so many colorful lines that zeroing in can sometimes prove difficult. Many of these elements, such as paints, wallpaper, towels, and accessories, are relatively inexpensive and can easily be changed.

One of the all-time favorite monochromatic options is the all-white bathroom. Beware, however, that even within the white category there are subtle variations, which run from a crisp milk color to a buttery tone. Mixing different whites together requires a deft hand to ensure that the combination looks like a deliberate choice

rather than an unfortunate mistake.

There are also monochromatic palettes that appeal to homeowners who want a bit more color. Some favor green in order to bring in the outdoors, some black to impart a sense of drama, and some gray or beige to inject sophistication.

For still others, bathrooms are the best places to let loose and have some decorating fun by mixing many different colors that may be considered too provocative to showcase elsewhere in the home, particularly in the more public spaces. In many cases, children's bathrooms are the best laboratories in which to experiment with a riot of colors, because kids remain the least inhibited guinea pigs when it comes to mixing and matching.

Opposite: CREATING THE SENSATION OF BEING IN A FISH TANK, THIS COLORFUL BATHROOM IS DECKED OUT IN SHADES OF AQUA AND ROYAL BLUE, WHICH APPEAR IN THE MIX OF GEOMETRIC TILES AS WELL AS ON THE PAINTED CABINETRY. A FEW ROWS OF YELLOW SUGGEST SAND OR SUN, DEPENDING ON ONE'S IMAGINATION. BLUE TOWELS AND A BLUE MIRROR FRAME FURTHER CONTRIBUTE TO THE UNDERWATER AMBIENCE. **Above:** BY ANGLING THE SHOWER AND SLANTING THE EDGES OF THE VANITY, THE OWNERS OF THIS ALL-WHITE MASTER BATHROOM WERE ABLE TO FIT ALL THE ACCOUTREMENTS THEY WANTED INTO THE NARROW SPACE. THE USE OF WHITE ON EVERYTHING FROM THE FLOOR TO THE CEILING ENLARGES THE ROOM VISUALLY, AS DO THE ALL-GLASS SHOWER STALL AND THE LARGE MIRROR ABOVE THE VANITY. ACCENTS OF BLACK ALONG THE EDGE OF THE VANITY AND AROUND THE RIM OF THE BASIN ADD DIMENSION.

Below: WORN WOOD PLANKING, PALE YELLOW PAINT ON THE UPPER PORTION OF THE WALLS, AND SOME STAINLESS STEEL TOUCHES HELP TO SOFTEN AN OTHERWISE VERY WHITE BATHROOM. DELICATE WHITE SHEERS BUNCHED TOGETHER AT THE WINDOW AND A SMALL BATH MAT ADD SOME TEXTURE AND CONTRAST TO THE OTHERWISE SMOOTH SURFACES OF THE ROOM.

Above: AN OLD-FASHIONED TUB WITH GOLD-PLATED FEET WAS PLACED ADJACENT TO A CURVING WALL OF WINDOWS THAT LOOKS OUT ONTO A PORCH AND THE WOODS BEYOND, OFFERING PLEASANT VISTAS. HINTS OF ROSE IN THE MOSTLY WHITE FLOOR TILES ARE PICKED UP BY THE OVERHEAD LIGHT FIXTURE AND THE FLOWERS.

Above: WHITE COMES IN VARIATIONS THAT RANGE FROM QUIET TO OBVIOUS, AND HERE THE GAMUT ADDS A RICHNESS THAT GIVES THE ROOM ITS REFINED YET LIVED-IN LOOK. IN THE CATEGORY OF ULTRAWHITE ARE THE PORCELAIN TUB, MARBLE FLOOR, SEMISHEER CURTAINS, PAINTED WALLS, AND CABINETS. MEANWHILE, THE UPHOLSTERED CHAIR SEAT, A BATHSIDE TABLE FOR RESTING A GLASS OF WATER OR A BOOK, A TERRY CLOTH ROBE, AND A TOWEL CASUALLY DRAPED OVER THE EDGE OF THE TUB INTRODUCE A SLIGHT CREAM SHADE. THE ONLY TRULY NONWHITE ELEMENTS ARE THE WOODEN MIRROR FRAME AND THE SUBTLE GRAY VEINING OF THE MARBLE COUNTERTOP.

Opposite: THE OWNER OF THIS BATHROOM/DRESSING SUITE PROUDLY DEBUNKED THE DECORATING ADAGE OF NOT USING TOO MUCH COLOR OR PATTERN IN

A SMALL ROOM. AS A RESULT, THE ROOM EXUDES A SENSE OF EXUBERANCE WITH ITS LIVELY RED-AND-WHITE PATTERNED WALLPAPER AND COORDINATING SINK

SKIRT AND SEAT CUSHION. THESE PROVINCIAL-LOOKING FABRICS PROVIDE A WELCOME SOFT COUNTERPOINT TO THE RICH POMPEIAN-RED TEXTURED DESIGN OF THE

DADO AND THE DEEP HUE OF THE CARPET. HORSE PRINTS REFLECT A FAVORITE PASSION OF THE WOMAN WHO USES THE ROOM. **Above left:** HERE,

THE MOOD IS CLEARLY TRADITIONAL, THANKS TO THE OLD-FASHIONED PEDESTAL SINK WITH GOLD-PLATED FITTINGS, THE ANTIQUE MIRROR, THE COLLECTION OF ARTWORK

AND CERAMICS, AND THE FAUX TORTOISESHELL FINISH OF THE UPPER WALLS. BUT IT WAS A LOVE OF COLOR THAT INSPIRED THE DEEP TURQUOISE HUE OF THE

WAINSCOTING AND THE TUB ENCLOSURE. A CRANBERRY-COLORED TOWEL ADDS A SPARK OF FESTIVITY. **Above right:** SELECTING A COLOR THAT WOULD MAIN-

TAIN THE RICHNESS AND DEPTH OF THE MAHOGANY CABINETRY, THE BLACK MARBLE COUNTERTOP, AND THE TUB SURROUND WAS A DIFFICULT TASK. THE OWNER

OF THIS SMALL BATHROOM SETTLED ON A RUSTY HUE, WITH A MATTE FINISH FOR THE DADO AND A FAUX MARBLE FINISH BEARING TOUCHES OF ROSE FOR THE UPPER

WALLS. VENETIAN BLINDS ADD A TRADITIONAL TOUCH AT THE WINDOW.

Below: TRANSFORMING THIS BATHROOM INTO A PIECE OF ABSTRACT ART, THE DESIGNER STAINED THE CABINETS AND DRAWERS OF THE VANITY WITH DIFFERENT SHADES OF RED, GREEN, AND OCHER, WHICH ADD UNUSUAL ZIP TO THE SPACE. THE WOOD FLOORING WAS STAINED A DARK COLOR, SERVING AS A VISUAL ANCHOR, AND TWO LARGE MIRRORS WERE FRAMED IN PALE MAPLE FOR CONTRAST. THE COUNTERTOP IS ONE LONG EXPANSE OF GRAY MARBLE THAT BLENDS WELL WITH THE OTHER COLORS. **Opposite:** HERE, BLACK IS USED EXTENSIVELY TO INJECT URBAN SOPHISTICATION INTO THE BATHROOM OF A HOME LOCATED IN THE MIDDLE OF A RUGGED CANYON. THIS SENSE OF CONTRAST IS CARRIED OUT FURTHER BY PITTING THE BLACK TILES AND COUNTER- TOP AGAINST PALE WOOD CABINETRY. THE WINDOWS, WITH THEIR METAL GRID, HEIGHTEN THE URBAN SENSATION, DESPITE THE FACT THAT THEY OVER- LOOK A NONURBAN LANDSCAPE.

Above: COLOR CAN BE SUBTLE, AS EVIDENCED BY THIS GRAY AND PALE WOOD BATHROOM. GRAY MARBLE LINES THE FLOOR, THE TUB ENCLOSURE, AND THE WALLS TO CREATE A CALMING FEELING, WHILE A LONG, NARROW NICHE STORES GRAY-AND-WHITE STRIPED TOWELS THAT PROVIDE VIVID CONTRAST. GOLD DETAILING FOR THE SHOWER ROD, DOOR HANDLE, AND TILE INSETS ADDS A BIT OF GLITZ.

Right: WHITE AND BLACK CREATE A TIMELESS COMBINATION IN THIS BATHROOM THAT HAS A BIT OF AN ART DECO FLAIR. BLACK MARBLE ON THE FLOOR ANCHORS THE LARGE SPACE AND IS REPEATED ON THE COUNTERTOP. A CHECKERBOARD PATTERN RIMS THE CURVED SHOWER FLOOR WHILE A NARROW LINE OF DIAMONDS ZIPS ALONG THE SHOWER WALL, BENEATH THE WINDOW, AND AROUND THE WHIRLPOOL TUB, ADDING A BIT OF ZEST TO THE SPACE.

Above: A LOVE OF MODERN ART INSPIRED THE USE OF ABSTRACT PAINTED TILES ALONG THE FLOOR AND ON ONE WALL OF A GLASS-DOORED SHOWER. THE EFFECT IS SUGGESTIVE OF A JACKSON POLLACK PAINTING. BY COVERING THE OTHER WALLS WITH PLAIN GRAY TILES AND SELECTING A SIMPLE PEDESTAL SINK, THE OWNERS PREVENTED THE SPACE FROM BECOMING TOO OVERWHELMING.

Above: IN THIS PRETEEN'S BATHROOM, A COLORFUL FISH MOTIF IS REPEATED ON THE SHOWER CURTAIN AND ON THE WALLPAPER BORDER AT THE TOP OF THE STALL. THE TRIM AROUND THE SHOWER IS PAINTED A GLORIOUS BLUE-GREEN REMINISCENT OF CARIBBEAN WATERS, AND THE ARRAY OF TOWELS BRINGS TOGETHER ALL THE DIFFERENT COLORS OF THE WALLPAPER, SHOWER CURTAIN, AND RAG RUG.

Below: THIS SWEET BATHROOM, DESIGNED FOR TWO YOUNG BUDDING BALLERINAS, HAS GREAT STAYING POWER AND WILL CONTINUE TO BE APPROPRIATE YEARS FROM NOW WHEN THE GIRLS ARE OLDER AND THEIR INTERESTS HAVE CHANGED. THE GRAY-AND-WHITE CHECKERBOARD FLOOR IS QUITE GROWN-UP, AS IS THE DIAGONALLY STRIPED MAROON WALLPAPER. THE ONLY NECESSARY MODIFICATIONS WILL BE A NEW SET OF TOWELS AND A MORE APPROPRIATE CHAIR.

Above: MANY MANUFACTURERS OFFER SINKS IN THE CRAYON COLORS KIDS LOVE. HERE, BRIGHT RED LIVENS UP A TRADITIONAL SINK, AS DO MIS-MATCHED FAUCET HANDLES. TO ADD ADDITIONAL PIZZAZZ, THE FLOOR WAS LAID IN TILES THAT FORM A CRAZY PATCHWORK QUILT WITH THEIR ZANY MIX OF COLORS AND PATTERNS. THE BOLD MÉLANGE IS SURE TO DELIGHT YOUNG USERS, AS WELL AS THEIR PARENTS, WHO WILL APPRECIATE ITS DIRT-HIDING CAPABILITY.

SPALIKE RETREATS

When space is no object and the budget is generous, there is no limit to the options available today for decorating or remodeling a bathroom. Many overscale bathrooms are referred to as spas because these rooms promise the ultimate in comfort and sybaritic pleasure. Often they include amenities similar to those found at well-equipped health centers and gyms, thereby bringing the facilities and luxuries of the outside world into the home.

The more elaborate home spas include his-and-her toilet cubicles, double lavatories with generous storage, a tub raised on a platform or sunk into the floor, a walk-in shower with multiple water effects, exercise equipment, dressing areas, and sometimes even a sauna. If the space

exists, some people transform these rooms into something closer to a living space with comfortable seating, entertainment equipment such as televisions and stereos, and even small refrigerators. The most envied examples boast the additional luxury of opening onto a deck or courtyard.

Part of the secret to many of these rooms is found in the details, not just the amenities, for they provide that individual design stamp known as panache. Such decorative devices might include gold-plated fittings for a very luxe look, an assortment of lush plants to create an indoor oasis, or dazzling accent tiles that add some glitz. Together, the right fixtures and details can have a stand-up-and-take-notice effect.

Opposite: ABUTTING FRENCH DOORS THAT OPEN ONTO A DECK OVERLOOKING THE WOODS, THIS SPALIKE TUB WITH WHIRLPOOL JETS PROVIDES ITS OCCUPANTS WITH THE FEELING OF BATHING OUTDOORS. RIMMED BY THE SAME RUSTIC BRICK THAT IS USED FOR THE HOME'S GARDEN PATHS, THE TUB FURTHER SUGGESTS AN OUTDOOR RETREAT. PLANTS GRACE THE EDGE OF THE TUB, REFLECTING THE GREENERY OF THE HOME'S SURROUNDINGS. **Above:** NESTLED BETWEEN MATCHING LAVATORIES, A WHIRLPOOL TUB CONJURES UP THE IMAGE OF AN ANCIENT ROMAN SPA WITH ITS LUXURIOUS MARBLE SURROUND AND GOLD FITTINGS. BUT THIS BATHROOM IS NO LITERAL TRANSLATION. CONTEMPORARY AMENITIES INCLUDE WALL-TO-WALL CARPETING, A LARGE PICTURE WINDOW LEFT UNCURTAINED, GOOD ARTIFICIAL LIGHTING, GENEROUS STORAGE, AND A RUSTIC WOOD CEILING WITH DECORATIVE BEAMS.

Above: TAKING ITS CUE FROM THE SURROUNDING RUGGED HILLS, THIS DRAMATIC SPA FEATURES A MIX OF EARTHY MATERIALS: MARBLE SPORTING DEEP TONES OF BROWN AND BLUE, BLUE-GRAY CONCRETE, AND FROSTED GLASS TILES. THE OVERSIZE TUB-CUM-SHOWER OFFERS A PANOPLY OF FAUCETS, STEAM FITTINGS, AND HANDHELD SPRAYS SO THAT BATHERS HAVE THEIR CHOICE OF WATER EFFECTS—AS FINE AS A MIST OR AS DRENCHING AS A JUNGLE RAIN. THE PEAKED ROOF, INSET WITH GLASS, USHERS IN STREAMS OF LIGHT. **Opposite:** "UNIQUE" IS THE WORD MOST USE WHEN THEY VIEW THIS COMPARTMENTALIZED BATHROOM, WHICH IS ENVELOPED IN A WARM MULTITONED BROWN MARBLE THAT UNIFIES THE SPACE. A CURVING GLASS-BLOCK WALL ACTS AS A SCREEN BETWEEN THE DRESSING AREA AND THE MORE ELEMENTARY COMPONENTS OF THE BATHROOM, WHILE A SIMILAR BARRIER SEPARATES THE SHOWER AND TOILET. SWINGING DOORS REMINISCENT OF THOSE FOUND IN OLD SALOONS GIVE THE SPACE A WESTERN FEELING.

Below: TUCKED INTO A LARGE CORNER, A WHIRLPOOL TUB WAS RAISED OFF THE GROUND SO THAT THE BATHER COULD BEST ENJOY THE VIEW PROVIDED BY AN EXPANSE OF TALL, UNCURTAINED WINDOWS. ADDITIONAL WINDOWS ABOVE BRING WELCOME LIGHT INTO THE HIGH-CEILINGED ROOM, WHICH, WITH ITS BLUE-AND-WHITE COLOR SCHEME, CREATES THE SENSATION OF BATHING IN THE SEA.

Above: THIS OVERSIZE WHIRLPOOL TUB IS THE INDOOR EQUIVALENT OF A HOT TUB. CAPABLE OF ACCOMMODATING SEVERAL USERS SIMULTANEOUSLY, IT IS SITUATED BENEATH A SLANTED CEILING IN A COZY ALCOVE JUST BEYOND THE CONVERSATION AREA OF A FAMILY ROOM. A SKYLIGHT BATHES THE ROOM IN SUNLIGHT, WHILE NATURAL WOOD FLOORING AND TRIM COMPLEMENT THE DESIGN.

Below: WITH THE HELP OF A FREESTANDING VANITY CRAFTED FROM HANDSOME TEAK, HIS-AND-HER BATHROOMS WERE CARVED OUT OF A SINGLE SPACE. A VAST MIRROR SET WITHIN A BOLD BLACK GRID THAT HAS A CONTEMPORARY ORIENTAL FLAVOR PROVIDES A MEASURE OF PRIVACY FOR EACH SIDE WHILE ALLOWING COMMUNICATION BETWEEN THE TWO AREAS. AN ALVAR AALTO CHAIR AND TABLE ALLOW THE OCCUPANTS TO KEEP EACH OTHER COMPANY COMFORTABLY. OVERHEAD, A CIRCULAR SKYLIGHT BRINGS IN NATURAL LIGHT.

Above: THIS SPACIOUS BATHROOM, WHICH IS THE SIZE OF MANY BEDROOMS, FEATURES DISTINCT AREAS FOR BATHING, SHOWERING, AND PRIMPING. A TELEVISION MOUNTED OVERHEAD PERMITS USERS TO CATCH THE NEWS OR A FAVORITE SHOW, AND A HIGHLY EFFICIENT YET MINIMALIST-LOOKING STAND PROVIDES A RESTING PLACE FOR THE REMOTE CONTROL, AS WELL AS TOWELS AND A TELEPHONE. THE MOOD IS COOL AND SLEEK BECAUSE OF THE PRIMARILY BLACK-AND-WHITE COLOR SCHEME.

Opposite: CONCEIVED AS A TRUE BATHROOM GETAWAY, THIS ROOM IS LIGHT YEARS AHEAD OF MOST IN ITS AVANT-GARDE DESIGN. THE TWO LAVATORIES PRESENT A VISUALLY EXCITING JUXTAPOSITION, WITH THE BASIN OF ONE JUTTING OUT FROM THE WALL AND THE BASIN OF THE OTHER SUBMERGED IN A GLASS-TOP TABLE. A TUB SUNK INTO THE SLATE FLOOR INVITES WEARY BODIES TO COLLAPSE RIGHT INTO ITS SOOTHING WATERS, AND A NEARBY HEATED TOWEL RACK MAKES EMERGING EASIER WHEN THE REAL WORLD CALLS. AN OVERSIZE CHAIN AND PADLOCK SUGGEST A LONGING TO BE KEPT PRISONER IN THIS PLEASURABLE RETREAT. **Above:** ALTHOUGH THIS LUXURIOUS BATHROOM FOR TWO APPEARS TO DEMONSTRATE PERFECT SYMMETRY AT FIRST GLANCE, THERE ARE ACTUALLY SUBTLE DIFFERENCES IN THE CONFIGURATIONS OF THE STORAGE UNITS DUE TO THE DISTINCT NEEDS OF EACH PARTY. OTHER ELEMENTS OF SURPRISE ARE THE ELEVATED GLASS COUNTERTOPS, WHICH PROVIDE FULL VIEWS OF THE BASINS, MAKING THEM APPEAR AS GIANT GLASS BOWLS RESTING ATOP THE CABINETS AND DRAWERS. RECESSED LIGHTING MAINTAINS THE AREA'S SLEEK LOOK, WHICH HAS BEEN ACHIEVED THROUGH AN ABUNDANT USE OF GLASS.

Below: JUST THE RIGHT AMOUNT OF WOOD WAS USED IN THIS TWO-PERSON MASTER BATHROOM TO CREATE A SENSE OF WARMTH AND PERMANENCE WITHOUT MAKING THE SPACE SEEM TOO DARK OR FOREBODING. THE DARK WOOD CASINGS, BEAMS, AND CABINETRY ARE COUNTERBALANCED BY THE SOFT GRAY MARBLE USED FOR THE SINK COUNTERTOP, BACKSPLASH, TUB SURROUND, AND BUILT-IN SHELVES. A MIRRORED WALL AND BARE WINDOWS OPEN UP THE SPACE, PREVENTING IT FROM SEEMING CRAMPED WHEN BOTH PARTIES ARE PRESENT.

Above: INSTEAD OF BEING USED FOR PLANTS, A GREENHOUSE WAS RETROFITTED TO ACCOMMODATE A LARGE WHIRLPOOL. THE LOOK IS CRISP, WITH A WHITE TUB, WHITE CERAMIC TILES, AND WHITE LINEN SHADES. THE CHAIR ADDS A BIT OF WHIMSY WITH ITS PAINTED FACE AND WINGS.

Opposite: SOME OWNERS PREFER THEIR WHIRLPOOLS TO BE PART OF THEIR BEDROOMS. HERE, AN INDOOR GARDEN OASIS HAS BEEN CREATED AROUND THE BATHING AREA, WHILE THE SLEEPING AREA (REFLECTED IN THE MIRROR) IS SHROUDED IN RUSTIC WOOD, APPEARING IN THE FORM OF PANELING, MULLIONS, AND FURNITURE. WOODEN CEILING BEAMS BRING THE TWO AREAS TOGETHER, WHILE A SKYLIGHT AND PLENTY OF WINDOWS KEEP THE ENTIRE SPACE LIGHT AND AIRY.

Above: THIS MASTER BATHROOM TAKES MAXIMUM ADVANTAGE OF THE HOME'S LUSHLY LANDSCAPED PROPERTY. THE WHIRLPOOL TUB AND GLASS-DOORED SHOWER ARE SITUATED IN FRONT OF A GIANT PANE OF GLASS THAT LOOKS OUT ONTO A WELL-SCREENED COURTYARD. THE EARTHY TONES OF BOTH THE VANITY AND THE METALLIC COPPER TILES SPECKLING THE FLOOR, WALLS, TUB, AND SHOWER COMPLEMENT THE OUTDOOR VIEW.

Below: DEVOID OF ANY CURTAINS OR SOLID PARTITIONS, THE SHOWER AND TUB IN THIS RELATIVELY NARROW SPA ARE SEPARATED BY ONLY A SINGLE STEP. AN ASSORTMENT OF TERRA-COTTA TILES ENVELOPS THE SPACE, WHICH EXUDES A DEFINITE FAR EASTERN TONE. THE DIFFERENT SHAPES AND SIZES OF THE TILES ADD VARIETY AND TEXTURE TO THE MONOCHROMATIC SPACE.

Above: THIS BATHROOM MAY BE SMALL, BUT ITS PLEASURES ARE DOUBLED BY AN ADJACENT DECK. AFTER SOAKING UP SOME SUN, USERS CAN RETREAT TO THE INDOORS AND SHOWER OR BATHE AMID A WHITE TILED OASIS TRIMMED IN NATURAL WOOD THAT ECHOES THE DECK.

SOURCES

DESIGNERS

(page 6)
Lee Harris Pomeroy Associates,
    architects
New York, NY
(212) 334-2600

(page 9)
Country Floors Showroom
New York, NY
(212) 627-8300

(page 10)
Elizabeth Speert
Elizabeth Speert, Inc.
Watertown, MA
(617) 926-3725

(page 13)
Gayle Monahan, ASD
Monahan Design Associates
New Town, CT
(203) 426-3066

(page 14)
David Livingston
Mill Valley, CA
(415) 383-0898

(page 15)
Sharon Campbell
San Anselmo, CA
(415) 453-2323

(page 17, right)
Brian Murphy
Santa Monica, CA
(310) 459-0955

(page 21, left)
Scott Johnson, architect
Los Angeles, CA
(213) 933-8341

(page 22, left)
Penne Poole
Washington, D.C.
(202) 342-8300

(page 22, right)
Barbara Scarallo Design
San Francisco, CA
(415) 558-8774

(page 23)
John Saladino
New York, NY
(212) 752-2440

(page 24)
Tom Beeton
Los Angeles, CA
(310) 657-5600

(page 30)
Sig Bergamen
New York, NY
(212) 861-4515

(page 31)
William Diamond
William Diamond Design
New York, NY
(212) 966-8892

(page 36, left)
Johnson & Wazenberg
New York, NY
(212) 489-7840

(page 37)
Deborah T. Lipner
Deborah T. Lipner Ltd. Interior
    Design
Greenwich, CT
(203) 629-2626

(page 40)
Josh Schweitzer, architect
Los Angeles, CA
(213) 936-6163

(page 41)
Lloyd Jaffert, architect
Jaffert-Mueller Architect Inc.
Bloomington, MN
(612) 897-5059

(page 45, right)
Mulder/Katkov
Los Angeles, CA
(310) 391-0680

(page 46)
Laura Clayton Baker
Los Angeles, CA
(310) 573-1232

(pages 49, 63 right)
Kerry Joyce
Kerry Joyce & Associates
Los Angeles, CA
(213) 461-7808

(page 50)
Josef Pricci Ltd.
New York, NY
(212) 570-2140

(page 52, right)
Mark Mack
San Francisco, CA
(415) 777-5305

(page 53)
Hodgetts, Fung
Los Angeles, CA
(310) 829-1969

(page 56)
Dan Mathieu & René Robert
Boston, MA
(617) 426-3806

(page 60)
David Gray
Los Angeles, CA
(310) 394-5707

(page 62, right)
Chris Fasoldt, architect
Karin Thomas, designer
Camden, MN
(207) 236-6248

(page 64)
Michael Lehrer, architect
Lehrer Architects
Los Angeles, CA
(213) 664-4747

Joanne Belsen, designer
Los Angeles, CA
(213) 654-3253

(page 65)
James Gillan, architect
San Francisco, CA
(415) 398-1120

(page 66, right)
Van Martin Rowe
Los Angeles, CA
(818) 577-4736

(page 68)
Margot Alofsin
Los Angeles, CA
(310) 395-8008

(page 69, left)
Biben/Busley
Biben/Busley Architects
Claremont, CA
(909) 624-8601

PHOTOGRAPHY CREDITS

© Richard Bryant/Arcaid: 19, 48 left, 51 right

© Phillip Ennis Photography: 9, 22 left, 50

© Feliciano: 12, 25

© Tria Giovan: 2, 16, 18, 20, 21 right, 29, 34, 57 left

© Nancy Hill: 13, 37, 41, 58, 62 left

© Simon Kelly/Arcaid/Belle: 28

© David Livingston: 14, 15, 22 right, 36 right, 38, 42, 43, 44, 45 left, 47, 52 left, 54 left, 54-55, 59, 61, 65

© Michael Mundy: 30, 31, 36 left, 51 left

© David Phelps: 7, 26, 33, 63 top

© Eric Roth: 10, 56

© Tim Street-Porter: 17 right, 21 left, 24, 32 top (Grounds Kent Architects, Perth, Australia), 39 (Richard Neutra, Architect), 40, 52 right, 53, 57 right, 60, 66 right, 67

© Brian Vanden Brink: 17 left, 27, 35, 48 right, 62 right

© Dominique Vorillon: 23, 32 bottom, 45 right, 46, 49, 63 bottom, 64, 66 left, 68, 69 both

© Paul Warchol: 6

INDEX